It *Happened*
Just like That

A Collection of True Stories

WILLIE WRIGHT SR.

WESTBOW
PRESS®
A DIVISION OF THOMAS NELSON
& ZONDERVAN

WestBow Press books may be ordered through booksellers or by contacting:

WestBow Press
A Division of Thomas Nelson & Zondervan
1663 Liberty Drive
Bloomington, IN 47403
www.westbowpress.com
844-714-3454

Scripture taken from the King James Version of the Bible.

ISBN: 978-1-6642-3953-1 (sc)
ISBN: 978-1-6642-3991-3 (e)

Print information available on the last page.

WestBow Press rev. date: 07/08/2021

To my family.

Contents

Preface

*And the Lord answered me, and said, write
the vision, and make it plain upon tables,
that he may run that readeth it.*
—*Habakkuk 2:2*

This nonfiction book contains true stories of happenings in my life. The Lord wants me to tell the world of His almighty power working through His messengers, known as angels. We learn that God is a spirit, and we devoutly worship Him.

God is real because He is a miraculous God who can do all things. Therefore, I believe in Him, and you can believe in Him too. You must accept Him as Jesus Christ, our Lord and Savior.

When you begin to read these true stories, you will see and understand the miracles in this book.

How It Began

*Behold I send an angel before thee; to keep
thee in the way, and to bring thee into
the place which I have prepared.*

—*Exodus 23:20*

I held certain beliefs at the age of five, and one of those beliefs was there were no such things as ghosts walking in a cemetery at night or being in places some people claimed were haunted. This was not a ghostly problem for me at this young age.

One cold December night, I was sleeping in my grandmother's house, which was about one hundred years old, when something transpired. My mother and father were also living in this old house during this time.

Asleep in the middle of the night, with the bedcover pulled up to my shoulders to keep me warm, I went to sleep. All lights were turned off for the night. Later in the night, during the hours of darkness, a most memorable moment occurred when I felt someone pull the cover down from my shoulders toward my feet.

To my astonishment, I looked up to see what was going on, and I realized it was not my parents moving the bedcover. I saw an angel in the form of a human kneeling on the right side of my bed, staring at me. The head, shoulders, and the rest of its upper body were clearly visible to me. At that moment, I knew without a doubt who was physically removing my bedcover at a slow pace. It was an angel. This sighting in darkness looked white in form, with a human appearance.

Realizing after a short while what was beside my bed, I decided to call my parents, who were sleeping across the hallway, and asked them if they came into my room and pulled the bedcover off me. They said no. Of course, I already knew the answer. They told me they were not aware of anything, because they were asleep.

Prophetic experiences began to noticeably occur to me after encountering this real episode. These prophecies have been true each time.

Since that cold December night, God has prophesized to me many times in different ways through dreams, visions, and other communications. These were always done with pinpoint accuracy by angels.

Years later my grandmother's house burned down, but the memories of this event will live forever.

Gas Station

**During the year 1969, the price of gas was about thirty-five
cents per gallon. There was a gas station and a garage at the
end of the street where I lived.**

When I cranked up my car, I went to the end of the street.
There was a sign advertising, "If you can guess how
much gas it would take to fill your car within a penny, your gas
would be free." An angel told me to fill up my gas tank, and I
said okay.

I pulled into the station by the pumps and told the attendant
how much it would take to fill my tank. He wrote the amount
down in his notebook. He told me that he would pump the gas,
and I agreed. I was standing close by as he pumped. When the
tank filled, he said it would hold no more gas. I had told him the
exact amount of gas to fill my car. I thanked him and enjoyed
my free gas. By the way, my car was on empty when I arrived
there. Thanks to the angel!

After leaving, I said to myself, *When my car needs more gas, I am coming back for more.* Before I used my free tank of gas, however, the owner took down the sign for free gas. His advertisement did not work, because there was one person who would consistently get his gas free of charge.

Close to Home

For with God nothing shall be impossible.

—Luke 1:37

Sometimes accidents happen closer to home.

On this night, after working on the night shift for twelve hours continuously, I had driven from Greenville to Pelzer. I was almost home when I suddenly fell asleep at the wheel. With my car in driving motion while I was asleep, an angel opened my eyes in a second for me to avoid hitting a telephone pole head-on in Pelzer by inches. I can tell you I was wide awake for the remainder of my drive home. My car was not damaged, but it could have been a bad accident if it had not been for God's angel. Thank you, Angel.

Hospital Journey

*And the Lord said unto him, Peace be unto
thee; fear not; thou shall not die.*

—*Judges 6:23*

In 1969 there were three children of ours living in the household, along with my wife and me.

During the night, our son inhaled something. My wife told me that he started gasping for breath. I told her that we needed to rush him to the hospital. Quickly, we got in the car, with her holding him while I drove.

I noticed shortly after leaving that my car was low on gas; therefore we had to stop at the gas station. Fortunately, after stopping to get enough to get us to the hospital, I told the station owner, after paying, that I had to rush my son to the hospital and to call the rescue squad. I asked him to tell them that I will be driving at a high speeds. I then sped off with my emergency lights blinking and looked down at my speedometer, which showed I was driving over ninety miles per hour. During that time of night, traffic was lighter than in the day. About three miles from the hospital, there was a divided road, one on the left and one on the right, leading to the hospital. At this intersection, several highway patrolmen were waiting for me, not knowing which road I would take.

I continued with my speed and blinking lights. After arriving at the emergency room, the patrolmen came in quietly and asked if everything was okay. I told them everything was okay.

They soon left the emergency room. The emergency doctors treated my son and got his breathing back to normal.

Thanks to God for protecting us from harm on our way to the hospital, and thanks to the emergency personnel for returning our son to normalcy!

January 20, 2017

For we cannot but speak the things
which we have seen and heard.

—Acts 4:20

President Donald Trump was elected and installed in office as the next president, succeeding former president Barack Obama. I was at home on this day when an angel told me that President Donald Trump would be impeached during his third year in office, which would occur by December 31, 2019.

After the angel relayed this message to me, I felt I could tell others what was going to happen in three years. When an angel from God tells me something, it is going to happen. As a result, I always feel confident and relaxed about the forecast from an angel of God. God wants me to reveal to all that He is God Almighty and has all power in His hands. With obedience to him, that is what I am trying to do, because I promised to him that I would.

My Eyes Closed

And the angel that talked with me came again, and
waked me, as a man that is wakened out of his sleep.
—Zechariah 4:1

There are times and circumstances that a person will not forget. Why? Because it had been embedded in one's memory. There is a reason why one cannot forget. The Lord wants you to realize forever how his messengers, called angels, intervene at a split second to accomplish a supernatural and believing act.

I departed for home after my work shift, traveling in my car before daylight one morning at approximately four thirty. I suddenly fell asleep at the wheel.

An angel opened my eyes, and I found myself behind a car in from of me, only about a few feet away, about to turn off the highway. The angel told me to quickly turn my car to the left of the road to avoid hitting or crashing into the rear of that vehicle. I did just that, causing me to avoid an accident entirely. This situation occurred about seven miles from home. Had it not been for the angel opening my eyes, there definitely would have been a crash scene with injuries.

I thank you, Lord, for your messenger!

An Angel Told Me

And he said, the things which are impossible
with men are possible with God.

—Luke 18:27

During the early years of my marriage, in the sixties and seventies, I decided to sign up for school bus driver training to supplement my income at Palmetto High School, located in Anderson County.

My school bus supervisor was David, who owned a theater in Anderson, South Carolina. As bus drivers, we would get our paychecks by going to David's office at the high school on a monthly basis.

One morning it was time to pick up my check. I was at home when an angel told me that David would deliver my check to me at my home, thus saving me time going to the school. In the next sixty seconds, a car started blowing its horn in my driveway. I went outside, and as I approached the car, I said, "David, an angel told me about sixty seconds ago that you would deliver my paycheck to me at home this morning."

He was astonished and mystified that an angel had told me what was going to happen. I thanked David for delivering it to me. He said, "You were absolutely correct." This was the first and only time David made a delivery of such. He then left, driving away in his vehicle.

I regret to say that David, a fine gentleman, suffered a heart attack a few years later and died.

Visitation with Family

My wife and I decided to visit relatives, so we went to her sister's house, which was not far from ours. Her sister, Geraldine, had married Reverend Spurgeon Jr.

After being there for a while, and while I was sitting on the couch in the living room, a message came and told me when my cousin Mattie and her husband, Robert, would arrive. The message also told me the precise moment we would see them.

The distance from Pendleton, South Carolina, to Williamston was about fifteen miles. Of course, none of the other family members were notified or had been informed of their coming. I informed everyone at the house that Robert and Mattie would open the kitchen door at exactly 4:20 p.m., or within sixty seconds of the specified time.

There was an electric clock hanging on the wall above my head and the couch. It had a second hand on it, denoting seconds within each minute. The reason for the second hand on the clock being so important particularly now was because when a message is received from God it occurs within sixty seconds. Everyone waited in anticipation.

As the specific time on the clock approached 4:20 p.m., I got the attention of everyone in the house so that we could all see if the message would come true. At this moment, everyone got quiet, and we were all watching and focusing on the clock.

When the long hand reached 4:20 p.m., I emphasized at this moment to the family that Robert and Mattie would turn the doorknob on the kitchen door and walk inside.

The second hand on the clock had just reached 4:20 p.m., thus making the next minute crucial for a message of specific accuracy.

The seconds continued and approached the forty-second mark on the clock, when suddenly the doorknob started turning. Robert and Mattie entered the house at precisely the time told to me in the message from God.

Everyone in the living room was amazed and astonished, as they witnessed an event with complete accuracy in a timely setting.

It is almost unimaginable how I can be anywhere at any time when God comes to me instantly and delivers a message to me.

Some people do not believe until they can see something for themselves. Well, I have a lot of believers!

Unexpected

For he shall give his angels charge over
thee, to keep thee in all thy ways.

—*Psalm 91:1*

Many unexpected things have happened at Roadway Express. A new trucking terminal was built in Greenville. Employees of the company moved into this terminal after its completion. The new terminal doubled the size of the old one, which was located near Bob Jones University and the Shriner's Hospital in the city of Greenville.

Being a dock records Clerk at the time, there were times when I had to make a trip around the dock at each trailer loading door with my tally cart, calculator, and other necessities. My job was to keep up to date with the bills and amount of weight loaded on each trailer and to make sure that each freight shipment was correctly loaded for its proper destination on the newly built dock. We had what was called a dragline. Carts on this line were constantly moving around the dock, loaded with freight destined for many places throughout the United States and other countries.

I had just begun to tally freight at one of the loading doors, which was situated at the side entrance to the trailer. I was standing with my back to the trailer, head down, looking at the paperwork on the cart. The dragline was running. Suddenly, I heard a tow motor from the opposite side of the dock, with its gas pedal seemingly pressed down while it was speeding across the dock.

Unaware of what was going on, the driver on the tow motor had a long rug on the pole of the tow motor headed toward the trailer where I was standing. The driver had not raised the rug to the proper height so that it would be above the constantly moving carts while traveling between the moving carts on the dragline. Instead, he had the rug pole low while trying to move between the carts that had only narrow spaces between the floats.

Suddenly, something hit my tally cart with force and knocked me and the cart backward off the dock and into the trailer yard below, with me bouncing off a trailer before landing in the yard. As I tried to recover off the ground, I noticed a big bruise on my left shoulder. As I went backward, my left shoulder hit a steel beam support, thus avoiding hitting my head, which would have caused a more severe injury.

It was God who prevented harmful injury to me, or even death, at Roadway.

Thanks be to God!

It Came from an Angel

*Surely the Lord will do nothing, but he revealeth
this secret unto his servants the prophets.*

—*Amos 3:7*

There are several radio stations people can dial into, depending on which one is their favorite. It may be one that gives the current news, plays popular music, tells jokes, or whatever the station must broadcast.

Most of the time, I chose to dial in on the radio station WRIX in Anderson, South Carolina. Here I could listen to news and music and commentary. Sometimes people would call in to answer questions.

On this day, with my cellular phone by my side, I was listening to WRIX. During these moments of listening, as I usually do when driving, there were questions being asked. Anyone could call in to the station to give their answer.

On this particular day, they asked the following question: What was the lowest temperature ever recorded on Grandfather Mountain? Frankly, I did not know the answer. I knew the telephone number for call-ins if I knew the answer to the question.

Suddenly, God told me to call in and tell them that the

answer was negative thirty-two degrees Fahrenheit. I felt confident of the answer because I knew it was from God, who is perfect. I immediately dialed the telephone, hoping no one had answered the question before my contact with the radio station. Fortunately, no one had answered the question correctly.

The person receiving calls asked me for the answer, and I responded with the answer God gave me. The announcer asked me how I knew the answer. I replied God had given me the answer.

The radio announcer seemed to be in somewhat of a daze. He told me that my answer was correct and to come to the radio station at any time to pick up my prize. Since I was already in the Anderson area, I went and picked up my prize approximately thirty minutes later.

When you have faith in God, he will provide. Because of my faith in Him, He proved without a doubt to me what He could and would do. He wanted me to spread the word to others that God is real and almighty. Without Him, I could not have projected with accuracy.

Thanks to the angels of God.

Part of My Duties

The Lord is my strength and my shield; my heart
trusted in him, and I am helped: therefore, my heart
greatly rejoiceth; and with my song will I praise him.
—*Psalm 28:7*

As part of my job at Roadway Express, Inc., I was assigned to periodic yard checks of trailers out on the yard to see if there was any unknown freight that did not have any paperwork. There was a rule that any raised door on a trailer that was open on the yard had to be pulled down and closed properly. To do this, I would have to climb up on the rear of the trailer and then stand up to reach the cord on the back to close the door.

One day, while I was out in the yard checking, an open door on a trailer was spotted. So I climbed up on the rear of the trailer and reached up to grab the cord. Suddenly, the cord slipped out of my hand, causing me to fall backward out of the trailer, with several feet to descend before hitting the asphalt ground.

Some way and somehow, with God on my side, I descended toward the ground backward. While in the air for a short period of time, my body made a 180-degree turn, positioning my body to hit the ground with my face downward and not downward with the back of my head. With this force, I hit my mouth with the help of my two arms and hands that braced me, causing some loose teeth and bleeding.

After catching my breath, with no one around, I managed my way back up to the dock and reported this accident to the operations manager, Jim. He sent me to the emergency room at Greenville Memorial Hospital to be treated.

I thank God for guiding me while in the air falling backward, turning my body with a complete rotation of 180 degrees before hitting the asphalt. I continue to be amazed and thankful for God's lifesaving miracle.

Her Eyes Were Amazed

In the town Williamston, there is a school building that was once named Caroline Elementary and High School. I graduated from this school in 1955. After new and additional schools were built in the local area, this school was eliminated and later became a community center in the town.

I was elected to the position of vice president on the board of directors. This organization, known as the Williamston Action Community Club (WACC) receives its support from the citizens in the local and surrounding communities, including the town of Williamston.

During this monthly meeting, which was held during the evening, one of the ladies who attended the meeting approached me. She said, "There is a light on the left front of the building that has not come on for several days. We need to call the electric power company to see if they can restore the light."

At that moment, I thought about all the times at Roadway Express when lights would come on as I walked under them. So I told the lady, Sallie, that I would investigate. I immediately went over to the light on the outside of the building and stood under it for a few seconds.

As I walked toward Sallie, the light turned on. I told her that I appreciated her informing me of the broken light. Sallie was amazed and astonished. I told her we saved time by not calling Duke Power. Normally, we do that concerning the light.

Over the next several days, I checked the community center to see if that light was burning, and it continued to burn. We have witnessed marvelous things!

Coworker Witness

At Roadway Express, I worked as a density coordinator, which was a part of my job to inspect freight for correct labeling, weight, forward destinations, and correct descriptions on freight bills.

After reporting to work one morning at four thirty, I began to take my walk around the dock, looking and checking freight bills at each trailer dock stand located near the entrance to each trailer at the outbound dock. When leaving my first trailer and then going to the next one, I noticed an overhead light was off. As I walked under the light, it lit up and stayed on. I did not pay much attention, but I remembered what had happened to the light that morning.

It was on the next morning after reporting to work. I stated my routine of walking around the dock from trailer to trailer. Further down the dock, I noticed an overhead light off and not burning. I remembered what happened to the light that was off the previous morning. I decided to walk under the light to see what would happen. After walking under the off light, it immediately came back on in a few seconds. This started to become exciting!

As a matter of fact, from then on, when a light was off, I would go and walk under the overhead light. The light would come on every time, no matter where it was located on the dock.

Some of the dockworkers would approach me when they noticed a light off and not burning. They would ask me to walk over and stand under the specified light to see if it would come on without me touching a switch or anything.

The news started spreading around the freight terminal about my special "feats" turning on lights without touching a switch. It was not only amazing to me but to the dockworkers as well. They mentioned the fact that it must be something special about me. They had never seen anyone do such a thing before.

Several days later, I was beginning my four o'clock shift. As I walked down the steps from my new office to start my tour of duty on the dock, I heard Mike, the terminal operations manager, call me over to where he was standing. Immediately, I wondered what he wanted.

Mike told me that he had heard from various people that I could turn off lights back on again. At that moment, he pointed across the dock to a light off at the time. He asked me to go over and see if I could turn that one back on without touching anything. I said, "Okay, I'll be glad to do it." Mike wanted to see for himself if what he had heard about me is really true.

So I walked over and stood under the specific off light pointed out by him. The light came on immediately. I turned around and walked back to where Mike was standing. I told him the mission was accomplished. The light was on, and that was what he really wanted to witness for himself. He reacted with disbelief and astonishment at what he had just witnessed with his own eyes.

This was another example of wonders to perform with amazing results.

The Possible

When working in the dock offices at Roadway Express, both inbound and outbound offices had bulletin boards displaying truck drivers and their arrival times at the terminal.

One day, after an incoming truckload of freight had not arrived, God told me to call the dispatcher, who was in an office at the other end of the terminal. Gene was the line-haul dispatcher during this shift. I called him on the telephone and told him that a specific truckload was overdue. At that moment I asked him to look through his office window to see if the overdue driver was entering the doorway. He then looked and said that the driver I mentioned was just entering the office from the doorway while I was speaking, and he came to Gene's window to check in.

I called Gene from my office on a daily basis. God told me to tell him when each driver would be checking in at the terminal with him, and each time I was right.

One time when I called Gene, he said the truck driver was not at the window checking in at his office. I immediately told him to look out through his window toward the entrance door, because the driver should be approaching his dispatch window. Then Gene said, "You are absolutely right, because the driver is now opening the door as we speak and coming straight to my window." Gene asked me how I knew the precise timing of these truck drivers. I told him God told me so. Without God, I would not have known.

After several days passed, I stopped calling Gene. The answers were accurate within a window of only sixty seconds. Amazing!

Awaken from Sleep

Call unto me, and I will answer thee, and shew thee
great and mighty things, which thou knowest not.
—Jeremiah 33:3

It is important to follow a doctor's instructions. My doctor prescribed a blood-pressure medication on a daily schedule in order to regulate my blood pressure.

Once my supply had been completely exhausted, I decided to wait a few days before getting my medicine refilled at the pharmacy.

In the middle of the night, I suddenly woke up after what seemingly felt like a blood vessel in my head had burst. At that moment, I got out of bed, turned on the lights, and rushed to the bathroom. I spat some blood out of my mouth. I began to wonder what had happened to me, hoping it would not be serious. My thoughts told me that if I continued to see the presence of blood coming out of my mouth, then I would go to the hospital as soon as possible. Well, the blood seemed to stop. I decided to take my blood pressure using my home kit. When taking my blood pressure, my bottom number registered high as never before. So I decided to go to the doctor's office the next morning. After examining me, the doctor told me it was a miracle I did not have a stroke. He told me to never skip taking my blood-pressure medicine.

This episode made me realize the importance of obeying the doctor's medical instructions. I promised to always take my blood-pressure medicine.

It was God who prevented me from having a stroke, and I thank God for what He has always done for me.

A Voice from Him

Going to bed to enjoy a comfortable night of rest is the goal for most everyone.

On this night at home, I was awakened by a plain voice coming from the direction of the church cemetery located within the same city block where I lived. This voice was clearly my father, who has been deceased for several years, calling me by name. I immediately asked my wife, who was sleeping, "Did you hear my father talking to me?"

"No," she said. After all, she was asleep.

But the voice was loud and clear. This was a communication to me from my deceased father. It was amazing to receive communication from beyond the grave. I will never forget this communication from my father.

Eyes

In 1997 and 1998, I had a part-time job as a stainless cookware salesman. My supervisor, Jerry, called me late in the evening just before darkness and asked me to meet him about halfway between my house in Williamston and Anderson. Jerry lived just on the far side of Anderson. He wanted to get some paperwork from me to turn in before I saw him again at the next weekly meeting.

It had gotten dark in the evening, and I departed my home a little early so that I could stop by another place before meeting Jerry at the designated location—a gas station on I-85.

I wore eyeglasses while driving at night. While en route to meet him, my eyeglasses had fallen to the floor of my 1995 Ford van. I wanted to have clearer vision for driving. The road I took in driving was not so familiar to me, because I had not traveled it in quite some time. In the process of retrieving my eyeglasses, I approached a stop sign I did not see until it was too late. I was driving at forty miles per hour.

There were three cars traveling the road to my left on the

crossroad. They were a few feet behind each other and going in the same direction.

Suddenly, I realized there was going to be a wreck. As I crossed the road after running through the stop sign, my vehicle went in between the limited space between one of the cars without touching or even getting a scratch on any vehicle. I crossed a ditch and traveled into the yard of a resident. Looking ahead of me instantly was a tree. I hoped to avoid a head-on collision. I came to a stop on the left side of the tree without touching it. I backed out of the yard and continued to travel on to meet my supervisor. We met at the designated place on I-85 at the gas station.

My excitement was evident as I recalled the events to Jerry. I looked around my van and noticed there was not any damage done to the vehicle.

It was a miracle. Thanks be to God.

After returning home, I told my wife, Frances, about the miracle, and that was all well. No wreck, no injuries, and no damage to the vehicle. I continued to wonder how this happened.

Of course, the cars traveling on the crossroad probably were wondering what they saw when I crossed between them. It was not Superman, but it was me, guided by the hand of God.

Thanks be to God!

Answers in a Vision

*The Revelation of Jesus Christ, which God
gave unto him, to shew unto his servants which
must shortly come to pass; and he sent and
signified by his angel unto his servant John.*
—Revelation 1:1

In 2019, getting ready in the bathroom at home, an angel showed me a vision and told me to expect the results of a trial at approximately nine o'clock. It was a trial involving a member of the family in an accident when picking up a patient who was going to be discharged from the hospital.

Another vehicle ran into her vehicle while turning into the hospital driveway, and she was charged with failure to yield right of way. She insisted to the police that the other vehicle was nowhere in sight before she made the turn. In fact, the other vehicle had to have been speeding over the hill to suddenly hit the rear tires and rear side panel on her vehicle, since the rest of her car was in the hospital driveway. Points given would cause her insurance to increase.

She went to trial to plead her case because she knew she was not guilty. On that same morning, an angel gave me the results before the trial started. The angel told me in a vision that the trial would be acquitted.

Later that evening, I went to her house and told her what the angel relayed to me that morning. I was right about the angel's message. This family member was acquitted of the charge.

God's angel is *always* right.

The Superdome

*So then faith cometh by earing, and
hearing by the word of God.*

—Romans 10:17

In November 1999, after retiring from Roadway Express, I decided to take a trip to New Orleans, Louisiana, with my wife to see the annual football classic at the Superdome, featuring two outstanding rivals, Southern University and Grambling College, two competitive teams. This was a great opportunity and time to go there and enjoy ourselves.

I had planned several times to go back to Louisiana for a visit to my alma mater, Southern University in Baton Rouge, Louisiana. I graduated there in 1959 with a bachelor's of arts in secondary education.

We decided to driver our 1995 Ford van instead of flying or riding the train because we could see more on our own. We stayed there for almost a week, and this was the first time attending a football game in the Superdome in New Orleans.

The main reason why these two rival schools played in the Superdome was because it was a place that could accommodate more spectators.

At halftime the score was 31–10 Grambling. An angel told

me that I did not come to this football classic to see Southern University lose. With the first half of the game looking very dismal and bleak for Southern, an angel said they would come back in the second half of the game and beat Grambling, even with a twenty-seven-point deficit.

The second half began, and we started to relax. Southern started scoring, making the game more interesting and exciting. Southern came from behind to beat Grambling 37–31. My wife and I became more joyous because these results were what we wanted to see—victory for Southern University.

So true what the angel told me of the desired results. It was amazing each time something like this happened. The remaining days there were exciting and blissful as we traveled to Baton Rouge and visited Southern University. We had a safe and wonderful trip.

Truth at Scales

*My sheep hear my voice, and I know
them, and they follow me.*

—*John 10:27*

As I worked in my office on the dock at Roadway Express, there was a message sent to me from God. The specific message sent to me was to verify to man what God can do with His Word. While turning my head and looking out the window in front of me, to the right was a dockworker attempting to move some freight from inside the trailer backed up to the dock. I hear Jack, a dock supervisor, tell the dockworker to weigh those three pieces of sizeable freight that had to be moved by a tow motor because of their size and weight. They had to be put on the scales situated directly in front of my office window.

God suddenly told me what the total weight of all three pieces would be. I went out of the office and immediately approached Jack standing beside the scales, waiting for the freight to be weighed. Only one piece at a time could be weighed because of the scale's size. I said God just told me what the total weight would be, and he replied, "Really?"

I told Jack to get a pen and write down my answer. I told him to write 1,727 pounds as the total for the three pieces to be weighed. Jack drew a line under the weights for the three pieces, then added the total. Jack said, "Willie, that is exactly the total you gave me before weighing. It is amazing!"

I then told Jack that I have total confidence in what God tells me, and I am not afraid to let others see what God can do. God does not fail.

School Bathroom Light

After talking to some coworkers about the amazing and astonishing things that could happen and did happen at various places.

There was a bathroom near my classroom at the school, where I taught special education.

One day the custodian came to see about the light in the bathroom and said that she would have to replace that light because it had turned dim and seemed to be burning out.

I heard Joyce, the custodian, remark about the light. So I decided to see if my presence under the light would make a difference or influence the dimness of the bathroom light.

I walked into the bathroom, stood under the light, and in a few seconds the light became brighter. At that moment, I called one of my coworkers to come and watch the light get brighter as I stood under it until amazement and astonishment overcame my coworkers. They witnessed the fact that I had influence on the light bulb when I stood under it. After leaving, the next person who went into the bathroom told me the light was okay.

When the custodian came back to fix or replace the light, I told her it would not be necessary, because it was working fine. Of course, I told her the true story, and she became amazed and astonished of the fact.

More witnesses have seen things happen in my presence.

Help When Needed

Therefore I say unto you, What things so
ever ye desire, when ye pray, believe that ye
receive them, and ye shall have them.

—*Mark 11:24*

Hard times came on a financial basis—a lack of sufficient money to pay bills was very evident. During the 1990s, I had tried and wondered how to get enough money to take care and bring my bills up to a current status. The mortgage on the house was past due, and there was no money to pay it. I gave up and said, "I hope the Lord will intervene and help me out financially." Becaul could not see my house being foreclosed due to bills made that should not have made previously causing this financial situation to prevail. I just started relaxing, stopped worrying, and believed through faith that the Lord would get me out of this financial situation. So I did just that.

A few days later, a mortgage lender called me and asked if I needed any money. I was surprised but overjoyed at the asking. I told them the situation and then asked if they would loan me the money. If so, it would be greatly appreciated. The financial institution loaned the money to me.

Oh, what a big relief! The Lord was always there for me in times of hardship.

Thanks be to the Lord.

An Angel Provided
the Answer

Sanctify them through thy truth: thy word is truth.
—*John 17:17*

I have and have had many friends. One of my friends lived in the Five Forks area of Anderson County and married a classmate of mine who graduated with me from high school in 1955 at Caroline High School in Williamston, South Carolina.

Well, it was one night when Johnny was returning home when he had a car accident. The accident occurred not far from home during the night. He was transferred to the Anderson Medical Center in Anderson, South Carolina.

The news of this accident was revealed to my wife and I the night of the accident. We immediately got into our car and went directly to the hospital to see how Johnny was doing. The doctors said he was in stable condition.

At the hospital, we could enter the room where he was placed. Joined by other family members and friends, we all talked at a minimum to Johnny while he seemed to look at us.

When I reached the place where I could see him and get his reaction, something came to me, telling me that Johnny would not make it, even though everyone else thought he would recover from his injuries.

Outside the hospital, with several in a huddle talking of his condition and believing he would make it out of the infirmary, I came out verbally and told them I disagreed with their assessment and that something told me that he would not make it out of the hospital alive. I regretted to inform them of the sad news, which was the opposite of what they were saying.

My wife and I left the hospital and returned home that night. Shortly after returning home, a telephone call came and said that Johnny had just died.

Regardless of the situation, my predictions continued to be accurate.

I reminded the people of what I told them about Johnny, and they told me that I was right.

Thanks be to God and His angels.

It Was Rocking

But he saith unto them, it is I; be not afraid.

—*John 6:20*

My brother-in-law, MB Jr., came by our house one day to visit my wife and I where we were living at the time in the town of Williamston. He borrowed my wife's car to drive that night. She gave him permission to drive her car, and he departed later that night.

After going to bed and falling asleep that night, I was awakened to hear the rocking of the empty chair sitting in the den—the same chair in which Junior was last sitting in before leaving the house. I asked my wife, Frances, if she heard the chair rocking in the den. She replied that she did not hear the rocking.

The next morning, we were informed by an incoming telephone call that Junior was involved in a car wreck. He was partially submerged in a creek just off Liberty Highway in Anderson, South Carolina. As a matter of fact, someone passing in an automobile spotted the wreck off the highway that was partially visible due to brush and high weeds around the wreck area. Junior was transported to the Anderson Area Medical Center.

After visiting him at the hospital and seeing him in bad condition, I told everyone that Junior would be all right. This was an accident warning him to get right with God. He later improved and was dismissed from the hospital.

I Listened

That if thou shall confess with thy
mouth the Lord Jesus and shall believe in
thine heart that God hath raised him
from the dead, thou shalt be saved.

—Romans 10:9

It was a nice day in the late 1950s when I decided to go for a ride in the car my parents had purchased for me. My travel route was a highway leaving north out of Baton Rouge, Louisiana. Ahead on the highway in front of me, a car was traveling at normal speed. I started to pass it, when suddenly an angel told me not pass—just stay behind. I did just that because I was not in a hurry. In a few seconds, a car traveling in the opposite direction on this two-lane road did exactly what I would have done. Unfortunately, there was a head-on collision for that driver, who collided with the car in front of me.

I immediately pulled over to the left side of the road to a closed store. In the 1950s, there were no cell phones. I saw a telephone booth on the outside in front of the store. I got a dime from my pocket and inserted it in the telephone and made the emergency call for the rescue squad to come to the scene for help. Communication today is much more convenient and expedient.

Soon after my call, the rescue team arrived and transported the victim to the hospital.

The guardian angel kept me safe and secure with my obedience because it could have been me instead. This instant moment by the angel will never be forgotten.

Intervention from Disaster

For I the Lord thy God, will hold thy right hand,
saying unto thee, Fear not: I will help thee.

—Isaiah 41:13

The Lord works in mysterious ways. Early one morning at Roadway Express, I entered the terminal yard from the parking lot. On this morning, the weather was foggy, making visibility extremely poor. While walking about halfway to the building terminal, one of the switch tractors that moved trailers was headed straight toward me at the regular speed in this foggy condition.

At this moment, an accident seemed unavoidable. No telling what the consequences of a tragedy that would have been. Thank God that Bobby, who was a regular switcher, was sitting in the tractor while an amateur was training and learning to drive the switch tractor. The amateur driver did not see me walking in the heavy fog on the yard. Being alert, Bobby saw me and quickly diverted the tractor. Thanks again to Bobby and God for preventing a disaster.

Incidentally, the exact time of this incident—the hour and

minute—coincided with my sister Cynthia's time of death at the Anderson Medical Center a few months before. This was something to think about in relation to her death and my avoidance of tragedy through Bobby and God.

Dr. Martin Luther King Jr.

And he said, Hear now my words: if there
be a prophet among you, I the Lord will
make myself known unto him in a vision,
and will speak unto him in a dream.

—Numbers 12:6

A teaching job in elementary education was offered to me at a school in Abbeville, South Carolina, in the year 1968. Mendell, a coworker from Williamston, also taught at this school. Both of us decided to take turns driving to work each day, since the school was about forty miles from home. We thought it would be better for us economically.

One morning during the middle of February 1968, while Mendell was driving, I told him that I had a dream before awakening that morning. On April 4, 1968, a very tragic event would take place. When mentioning this to him that morning, it was almost two months later when this was supposed to take place. I wanted someone to remember what I predicted would happen.

When April 4 arrived, beginning that morning and throughout the workday, my dream of almost two months ago was on my mind, wondering if it would come true. There weren't any TVs or radios at the school to watch or listen to like we have today, nor were there any available for use nearby.

As I returned home on April 4, 1968, I asked my wife if she had heard any unusual news that day. She said no. Of course, at that time, the TV was turned off, and she was preparing food in the kitchen. At that moment, I said okay. Then I immediately went to the den, where the TV was, and turned it on. After sitting in the rocking chair for a few moments, a breaking news story appeared on the screen. It read "Dr. Martin Luther King Jr. was assassinated today in Memphis, Tennessee." I relayed the news to my wife in the kitchen and told her of my dream in February, even though it had to be tragic.

Traveling to Work
with Visions

And the vision of the evening and the morning
which was told is true: wherefore shut thy up
the vision; for it shall be for many days.

—*Daniel 8:26*

On the way to work early one morning to start my 6:00 a.m. work shift, there were remarkably interesting moments on the way. When I was only 2.2 miles from reaching my destination, a marvelous thing occurred.

A lighted neon sign suddenly appeared ahead and in front of me. On this lighted sign there were three names appearing, with only one name in bright light, whereas the other two names were listed in plain sight, with a darkness of shade over them. This person's name, Sam, stood out with brightness, which made it very distinguishable from the other two.

Sam was the terminal operations manager at the time. He was one of three candidates who were seeking a job as a sales representative at Monroe, North Carolina, which was a satellite or branch of Roadway Express in Greenville, South Carolina.

During the following days, practically everyone at Roadway

Express in Greenville was debating as to who was going to be selected for that sales job in Monroe. Actually, no one knew. They were only trying to guess who might be chosen.

After reporting to work that morning, I told my fellow workers that I knew in advance the person who would be selected and get the job. Everyone asked me how I knew. I told them that a vision came and appeared before me that morning on the way to work.

My coworkers asked me to tell who it might be. I responded by telling them that I would not reveal the answer until a few days before the selection.

I just listened to my coworkers as days passed, and we talked about the selection. As for me, I had already predicted the selection but kept it to myself. After all, I wanted to see if a vision of mine would come true.

Sam, terminal operations manager, tried to get me to tell him in advance who would be the choice, but I refused to even give him the answer.

My shift during this time was referred to as seven on and seven off. On this schedule, a person would work seven days and be off the next seven days. Each workday would consist of twelve hours.

It was during my last shift of the week before selection—namely, on a Sunday before going on a week's break. The selection was to be made on the following Thursday.

I decided on my last workday to reveal the answer. It was approximately one hour before the end of the shift when I approached Sam in his office. I reached out to shake his hand, congratulating him on being selected for the vacant position the following Thursday, as though the decision had already been made, but it had not been made at this time. I told him if he did not get the position this would be the first time of which I would confront failure from a vision. I asked him to give me his home telephone number in case I wanted to call him, and he did so.

When the next Thursday morning arrived, I telephoned Roadway Express and asked to speak to the terminal's secretary, Bernice. I asked her, "Who got the sales representative job in Monroe?"

Bernice replied, "Sam."

"Thank you," I said and hung up the phone.

I immediately found Sam's home telephone number and dialed. He answered the phone and said, "You were right, Willie, in your vision."

I congratulated Sam again.

Credit goes to the vision!

Little League
Football Game

The day was ordinary, except for what was to transpire later in the evening. My grandson was an eight-year-old football player who played with a local team in Pelzer, South Carolina. This football team had a scheduled game to play in Belton, South Carolina.

Families and others associated with or connected to the football players would follow and support the players when they were schedule to play, whether at home or away. This meant a lot to the young players, knowing they were supported by home folks.

It was on a Friday during football season when our family traveled to Belton, only a few miles away, to see our grandson play in the game as a running back with the team. I was standing on the sidelines during the fourth quarter of the game, with only a few minutes remaining. The opposing team was leading by a small margin. An angel told me, and I knew that, on the next play of the game a player on our team would get the ball and run all the way down the field for a touchdown, and we would win the game.

You see, I was foretold what would happen near the end of the game. An angel was precise and with the accuracy that has been, and continues to be, amazing. No matter where I might be or what time it might be, it is always before the happening.

Television Show

M any people watch television. Of course, there are a variety of programs and show for viewers to choose.

When I was sitting in the den at home with my family and others, a particular show was on. It was remarkably interesting to us on this night. The name of the show was *The Price Is Right*. The announcer had a lady standing near him, and a brand-new car was visible on the stage. If she could guess the price of the vehicle, she would win the car.

An angel told me the lady would not guess the correct price, but if I were on the show, my answer would be correct, thus winning the car. The angel gave me the answer.

I told my family and the others about my wishing to be on the show. So they listened carefully and watched the show to see who had the correct answer. I told everybody what the correct price would be for that brand-new car. We all waited patiently and attentively.

The lady on the show gave her answer, but it was wrong. The announcer told her the correct price, which was exactly the price that was told to me moments before by the angel: $7,498.00.

I immediately arose out of my seat on the couch and exclaimed that if only I had been on that TV show I would have won the nice new vehicle. All those around said that my price was right, to the dollar.

I have always said that angels tell me what to expect, and the angels were always correct, no matter what the circumstances may be. All credit goes to God's angels.

Our United States President

*Have not I commanded thee? Be strong
and of good courage, be not afraid, neither
be thou dismayed: for the Lord thy God is
with thee whithersoever thou goest.*

—Joshua 1:19

W*e have had several United States presidents take office after
winning political elections during my lifetime. This president
was Richard Nixon, who belonged to the Republican Party. Of course,
party lines do not have anything to do with this writing.*

Nixon, in August 1973, went on national television to deny
any involvement in the Watergate scandal.

I happened to be in my bedroom at home the day Richard
Nixon appeared on national television to deliver his address. As
I looked into the president's eyes and face on TV, an angel said,
"Nixon is telling a lie." Some people may have believed him, but
not me.

I immediately went to the kitchen in the house, where my
wife, Frances, was and told her that Nixon just told the American
people a lie, but not to me. I told her an angel relayed to me that

Nixon would do one of these things soon while in office: he would resign from office before the end of his term, or he would be impeached. I told my wife to remember what I had told her because an angel told me this was going to happen.

On August 8, 1974, Richard Nixon went on TV to announce that he would resign from the presidency the next day at noon.

So Richard Nixon resigned from office before being impeached. I told others what would happen before Nixon's resignation became official. Remember, the angel of God revealed to me what would happen before it happened. Angels of God never fail to give me the correct answers to the future.

The Computer

The Internal Revenue Service of the United States government is known by every American citizen who prepares and turns in an annual tax return.

It was for me, just before the April 15 deadline, to get H&R Block to prepare my tax return. My wife and I both entered the tax agency for preparation of forms to be mailed before the tax deadline.

The tax preparer, a lady, was sitting in front of her computer, filling in the required figures and information, when suddenly the computer started acting up and not working properly. The lady told us that this was the first time her computer had done something of this sort. She wondered what was going wrong.

At this moment, an angel told me that if I would go outside of the office for a brief period, like two or three minutes, then the computer would start functioning again like normal. This was happening because I was standing beside the computer.

I immediately told her that I would step outside the door for a brief time and then return. After returning to the office, the lady said that the computer started back up as normal after I departed from the office.

I realized that what the angel told me to do was correct.

The Night Before

There are many things that can occur during the night. It was in December 2009 when I had a dream during the night. It showed me that soon there would be change in my position as an assistant teacher at the high school in Williamston, South Carolina, where I worked with others in special education. The dream told me that I would be called into the principal's office and be reassigned to another position in the school.

Well, on Friday, December 4, 2009, at approximately 2:00 p.m., the teacher with whom I worked informed me that the principal at the school wanted to see me in the office at 2:30 p.m. I immediately wondered why I was being called to the office. My mind referred me quickly to my dream the night before, which was on Thursday, December 3.

After arriving in the office at 2:30 p.m. to meet with the principal of the high school, I was informed by him that he had a reassignment for me. It was to begin Monday, December 7, in another phase of special education at the school. I would be assigned to a special student who would be transferred to a different section in the school on that date.

My dream of the night before came true. It was amazing how these dreams came to fruition. It was not by dreams alone but by God.

Examination Score

When I was teaching in the public schools during my early years of marriage, South Carolina teachers were paid compensation according to their score on the National Teachers Examination. During this time, I already had a grade of B on the examination, but I felt as though I could make an A on the exam.

One morning, on the scheduled day for the next National Teachers Examination test to be given in Greenville, I decided to take the test. On this January morning, the weather was bad. It had snowed and sleeted the night before, making driving hazardous.

The distance to travel to take the test was fifteen miles from Williamston to Greenville. The road was covered with sleet, ice, and snow. I was driving slowly, about eighteen miles per hour, behind a Greyhound bus leaving the town of Pelzer. Suddenly, my car started veering to the left side of the highway. I wondered if there was a vehicle approaching from the opposite direction because the bus in front of me obstructed my view of oncoming traffic. Luckily, as I veered toward the left side of the road, there was no vehicle approaching from the opposite direction.

Instantly, an angel told me that the brakes on my car would not help me due to the ice on the road. That angel told me to turn my steering wheel to the right, which would cause the back end of the vehicle to swirl around and bring my car to a stop. If it did not stop at the edge of the cliff in that manner, then I should immediately jump out or get out of the car somehow before it plunged down a steep embankment, thus trying to avoid serious injury.

I did that in about two or three seconds. My car swirled with the back end stopping at the edge of the cliff on the opposite side of the road. I got out of the car after coming to a complete halt and saw that the back wheels of the vehicle were only about two feet from the edge of the cliff.

I did not get nervous, because quick thinking that came to me at the spur of the moment prevented that from happening. I got back in my vehicle and headed toward Greenville to take the National Teachers Examination.

A little while later, while en route to Greenville, I started to get a little nervous thinking about what had happened that could have led to serious injury. After arriving in Greenville safely and on time that morning, I proceeded to take the exam. My performance and results were astonishing. I made an A on the exam, despite what I went through before the exam that morning.

Thanks be to God, who always guides and makes the right decisions.

Episodes at Three Restaurants

*If any of you lack wisdom, let him ask
of God, that giveth to all men liberally, and
upbraideth not; and it shall be given him.*

—*James 1:5*

During our return from Louisiana, my wife and I were visiting and traveling from place to place in my own vehicle. There were moments when it was time to eat, no matter which meal it was, or simply a taste for something special, even it was gumbo in the French or pelican state known as Louisiana.

On the way from New Orleans to Baton Rouge, we decided to stop at a restaurant. After entering the restaurant, we ordered. We waited patiently while our food was being prepared. Suddenly, a waitress came out of the kitchen with the tray in her hand, and she dropped the tray of food intended for us. The waitress said, "This is the first time I have ever dropped a tray of food like this, but I will prepare another tray for you."

After the second tray was prepared, the waitress came out of the kitchen—this time without incident—and safely laid the tray on the table before us. She apologized for the incident. We told her everything was okay.

After we finished eating, we left and continued heading to our destination of Baton Rouge. While on the way, we discussed the incident that happened at the restaurant we had just left.

The very next day, we stopped at another restaurant. We placed our order with the waitress. She said, "It will not take a long time to prepare your order," and that she would return shortly.

As we sat at the table while our food was being prepared, we discussed what had happened at the previous restaurant, wondering and hoping that the same incident would not occur again this time.

The waitress came out of the kitchen with our food. About halfway toward us, she dropped the entire tray of food. She said to us, "I am sorry that I dropped your food. I do not understand it, because I have never done this before since working as a waitress. You will be served another tray of food. Sorry about the incident."

The waitress went back into the kitchen. We discussed the similarity of circumstances occurring in different restaurants with different people. What a correlation that was happening wherever we went.

She came out of the kitchen and placed the tray of food on our table, apologizing for what had happened to the previous tray of food. We enjoyed our food without incident.

We decided to leave and continue our sightseeing in Louisiana. On the last day of the week, we were leaving New Orleans, where we had been staying not far from the Superdome. We decided to stop at a restaurant in Slidell to eat our last meal— one we had never been to before.

After entering, we gave our order to the waitress. She then

went into the kitchen to prepare our order. While waiting, we discussed again what had happened to the other waitresses in the previous two restaurants. We wondered if it were possible that the same thing would occur for the third time at this restaurant.

The waitress came out of the kitchen. Halfway to us, she dropped our tray of food! With astonishment, she shook her head and said, "I cannot believe I dropped this tray. It has never happened to me. I just do not understand and do not want to believe I dropped it. I am sorry this happened. I will get you another tray of food."

While the waitress was in the kitchen, we could not believe that similar circumstances had happened in three different locations in Louisiana involving different people unknown to each other.

The waitress returned with our food and was being extracareful. After we finished eating, we said it was time to keep moving out of Louisiana before a fourth similar incident happened again for some reason.

It must have been something about me that triggered all three incidents—that is, some sort of radiance or something maybe like the lights coming on during my presence. Maybe one day the mystery of these occurrences being so similar will be researched.

As we continued our way home, there weren't any more of these incidents, for which we were glad.

God in Control

*The name of the Lord is a strong tower: the
righteous runneth into it, and is safe.*
—*Proverbs 22:19*

*I*n my later years at Roadway Express, in 1996, while working on the
night shift, 10:30 p.m. to 7:00 a.m., my head seemed to be clogging
*or stopping up with something like a sinus infection. About the middle
of my shift, I decided to take half of a medicine tablet that I saved in a
bottle for some years because it was so effective. It had relieved me in
about two hours from the same condition that I was feeling at this time.*

I finished my shift and departed for home—fifteen miles
away. About two miles from home, I started to get sleepy while
driving my pickup truck. I was battling to keep my eyes open on
Highway 20, leading toward the town of Pelzer, South Carolina.
I suddenly went to sleep at the wheel while beginning to round
a curve. My truck traveled, without me in control, down and
around a steep curve before crossing the Saluda River bridge,
which separated Anderson County from Greenville County.

My truck continued traveling up the road, approximately one
thousand yards, still with me asleep, before veering to the right
side of the road. As it began to veer off the road into some high
grass, my eyes began to open. I did not know my whereabouts

on Highway 20. The only thing that came to mind as I left the highway was the movie *Twister*, because of the high weeds and grass. In front of me, I could see a telephone pole. As I headed toward it, with a short distance to go before hitting it, there was no time to avoid an accident.

A passing motorist saw me after the accident and called the rescue squad to take me to the Anderson Medical Center in Anderson. This motorist had a cellular phone from which to make the emergency call. I was fortunate. I had no broken bones. I did not collide with any oncoming traffic as I traveled along and around various curves going downhill. I crossed the bridge safely before coming to a stop at the telephone pole.

It was God who had control of my truck from the moment I fell asleep until I collided with the pole. The circumstances could have been worse. God made sure everything was in His hands—that is, He was the one and only one who drove the truck that distance. Every time I passed that section of highway, it would always amaze me how God can take control, making everything much better. I will always give credit to God for always taking care of me.

A Vow to Be Kept

*If a man vows a vow unto the Lord, or swear
an oath to bind his soul with a bond; he shall
not break his word, he shall do according
to all that proceedeth out of his mouth.*

—*Numbers 30:2*

On March 26, 2020, an unusual time for me to lose my appetite, I did not feel like eating any food.

On March 27, my temperature seemed to rise. My stomach became upset, and I didn't want to do much of anything.

On Saturday morning, March 28, as I attempted to get out of bed and sit up, I could not because of being too weak. I could not stand, and I became helpless.

My son is a truck driver, so I called him to come over to my residence and help me out of bed. I thought he might have been home for the weekend, but instead he was trucking in another state. He then called my daughter, who lived in town, to call the paramedics for emergency help. Other members of the family responded too. Only the paramedics could help. Two emergency vehicles arrived with two paramedics in each vehicle. They rushed inside and said the best thing for me to do was to let them take me to the hospital because of my condition. I told them what hospital to take me to. They said okay. It took all four paramedics to pick me up and put me on a stretcher to be rushed to the emergency vehicle. Remember, during this time, I was helpless. After they put me inside the ambulance, I prayed silently to the Lord to let me live because I wanted to spread the Word to all on earth.

"I know this is a time when the COVID-19 virus has spread globally across the world to the United States and that so many people have died from this outbreak. I promise you, Lord, I will do what you ask of me!"

I was taken to the Greenville Hospital, where they took me in immediately because I had COVID-19 symptoms. They treated me consistently, and I was put in a private room. In this room, nurses and doctors entered wearing masks, but no N95 masks, because they did not have any at that time. After leaving the room, they would take off their protective gowns and gloves and discard them in a trash can.

On April 2, 2020, after I had been given a virus test, the results came back negative. Then the hospital released me to go home.

Thank you, Lord! I will keep my promise to you!

My Prayer

Dear Heavenly Father, I give praise to you and your angels, who are your messengers that prophesized of things that could come in the future.

Your angels were always right, in visions, dreams, and in communications with me. I did not have a doubt about communication from your angels at any time. That is why I believe in you, and that you are the Almighty God of the world and its people. I pray that unbelievers will believe in you, God.

We worship you, God, in spirit and in truth. God, I know you want me to spread the Word to all that you are real. Amen! Amen!

—Willie Wright Sr.

Printed in the United States
by Baker & Taylor Publisher Services